◆ SECTION 1:

WAYS IN WHICH CORNISH NAMES

Cornish place names fall into 4 mai[n]

1a. Names consisting of a single word.
1b. Names consisting of a noun with the definite article.
1c. Names consisting of a noun with an adjective.
1d. Names consisting of two nouns.

(The wide range of variation in spelling of place names elements in Cornwall, and hence the need for a modern standard form, is demonstrated in Section 2; many places names have been badly corrupted over time and may not be immediately apparent.)

1a. The name can be a single word, a noun:

OS Map	Cornish	Meaning	Cornish root
Hayle	Heyl	estuary	[heyl]
Heskyn	Heskynn	sedgemoor, marsh	[heskynn]
Ince	Ynys	island, isolated place	[ynys]
Landrake	Lannergh	clearing	[lannergh]
Looe	Logh	inlet	[logh]
Par	Porth	cove	[porth]
Praze	Pras	meadow	[pras]
Rose	Ros	promontory, moor	[ros]

1b. A place name can be a noun with the word an *(= English 'the') put before it:*

This word **an** changes the initial letter of the following word in many cases, according to the following scheme:

B becomes V	C/K become G	CH becomes J
D becomes TH[1] (soft)	GW becomes W	G becomes W or disappears
M becomes V	P becomes B	T becomes D

[1] written as **DH** in Cornish and pronounced like the soft *TH* in English 'the', 'this' etc.. This is called mutation (soft mutation or lenition) shown here as ² and which occurs in other

circumstances as well and in all the six Celtic languages (Breton, Cornish and Welsh - the Brythonic group - and the Gaelic group of Irish, Manx and Scottish Gaelic).

OS Map	Cornish	Meaning	Cornish root
Angarrack	An Garrek	the rock	[an+²karrek]
Angrouse	An Grows	the cross	[an+²krows]
Drift	An Drev	the settlement	[an+²trev]
Ninnis	An Ynys	the island	[an ynys]

1c. A name can be a noun with an adjective:

Both the adjective and the noun may be mutated. In Cornish place names the noun and adjective are normally written as one word. The adjective usually follows its noun.

OS Map	Cornish	Meaning	Cornish root
Andrewartha	Andrewartha	the top settlement	[an+²tre+²gwartha]
Camborne	Kammbronn	crooked hill	[kamm bronn]
Carthew	Kardhu	black fort	[kar+²du]
Halwyn	Halwynn	white down	[hal+²gwynn]
Hendra	Hendra	old settlement	[hen+²tre]
Parknoweth	Parknowydh	new field	[park nowydh]
Penzance	Pennsans	holy head	[penn sans]
Porthmeor	Porthmeur	big cove	[porth meur]
Redruth	Rysrudh	red ford	[rys rudh]
Retew	Rysdu	black ford	[rys du]
Trevean	Trevyghan	small settlement	[tre+²byghan]
Trenouth	Trenowydh	new settlement	[tre nowydh]
Trewartha	Trewartha	top settlement	[tre+²gwartha]

The adjectives **hen** ('old') and **kamm** ('crooked') are unusual in that they come before the noun.

1d. A name can consist of two nouns:

This is probably the commonest form of Cornish place names. We have to interpret it as 'the **something** of or by or on or with **something**'. Again when these occur as a Cornish place name, they are written as one word.

A backgrouond to Cornish, an occasional series, number two

THE FORMATION OF CORNISH PLACE NAMES

Graham Sandercock
Wella Brown

Kesva an Taves Kernewek
The Cornish Language Board
© 1996

ISBN 0 907064 63 9

THE FORMATION OF CORNISH PLACE NAMES

Many students first take an interest in the Cornish language through studying place names. This paper is a brief introduction to how Cornish place names are formed and gives some selected examples. However for the serious student attention should be drawn to more authoritative works, particularly the recent work of Oliver Padel.

In the lists which follow, the usual map form of the name is shown in *italics*, the Cornish language form is shown in **bold** and the English meaning follows. The Cornish word root is shown in square brackets [ ].

The spelling of Cornish names are given in *Kernewek Kemmyn* and to those who find the Cornish forms unfamiliar, remember that bi-lingual forms of place names are found in many societies where two languages are in operation, for example amongst our near neighbours in Brittany and Wales.

Indeed many English versions of names are variants on the original language:

Moskva/Moscow,
München/Munich,
Beograd/Belgrade,
København/Copenhagen,
Lisboa/Lisbon,
Caerdydd/Cardiff,
Al Qahira/Cairo
Rosko/ Roscoff,
Bosvenegh/Bodmin.

In Cornwall it is unlikely that the well known but anglicised, often corrupted forms of Cornish names will disappear but let us at least allow for the co-existence of both.

OS Map	Cornish	Meaning	Cornish root
Cargreen	Karrekreun	rock of a seal	[karrek reun]
Egloshayle	Eglosheyl	church by estuary	[eglos heyl]
Kelly Bray	Kellivre	copse on a hill	[kelli +²bre]
Langore	Nansgover	valley with stream	[nans gover]
Millendreath	Melindreth	mill on beach	[melin+²treth]
Polgooth	Pollgoedh	goose pool	[poll goedh]
Polventen	Pollfenten	pool by spring	[poll fenten]
Portloe	Porthlogh	cove by an inlet	[porth logh]

This type of place name is very common.

Very commonly too the second element is a personal name of a chief, king, saint, missionary or pioneer farmer. Although some are known or can be identified or can be worked out by analogy with Welsh or Breton parallels, many of these personal names have long since fallen out of use or are, at best, very obscure.

OS Map	Cornish	Meaning	Cornish root
Bossiney	Boskini	Kini's dwelling	[bos Kini]
Carworgie	Karworgi	Gorgi's hillfort	[ker+²Gorgi]
Egloskerry	Egloskeri	Keri's church	[eglos Keri]
Launceston	Lannstefan	Stephen's holy site	[lann Stefan]
Lelant	Lannanta	Anta's holy ground	[lann Anta]
Liskeard	Lyskerrys	Kerrys' Court	[lys Kerrys]
Trago	Trejago	James' settlement	[tre Jago]

The two nouns may be joined by **an** ('the') and conventionally now written as separate words. The English 'of' is not expressed in Cornish.

OS Map	Cornish	Meaning	Cornish root
Castle an Dinas	Kastell an Dinas	castle of the fort	[kastell an dinas]
Crows-an-wra	Krows an Wragh	cross of the witch	[krows an+²gwragh]
Pedn an Drea	Penn an Dre	end of the town	[penn an+²dre]
Parkandillack	Park an Deylek	field of the dungheap	[park an+²teylek]
Ponsanooth	Pons an Woedh	bridge of the goose	[pons an+²goedh]
Praze an Beeble	Pras an Bibell	meadow of the pipe	[pras an +²pibell]

◊ ◊ ◊ ◊ ◊ ◊

SECTION 2:

COMMON PLACE NAME ELEMENTS

The above mentioned methods of forming place names are the chief ones. To reach a full understanding of the meaning of a name, we need to know the meanings of all the words, including personal names, which make up the name. This often causes some difficulty but as a starting point we can identify certain common nouns and adjectives, a knowledge of which will permit at least a part of many names to be understood. Remember that the first letter of the noun or adjective may have undergone mutation as in Section 1b above and that adjectives follow the noun, except **hen** ('old'), and **kamm** ('crooked') .

◊ ◊ ◊ ◊ ◊ ◊

The following common place name elements are divided into four sections.

    2a. Nouns which mean a habitation or settlement.
    2b. Nouns denoting man made features.
    2c. Nouns denoting natural features.
    2d. Common adjectives in place names.

In the following lists the Cornish language element is given first in **bold**. This is followed by the various spellings of the element as found on maps. The wide variety of forms found reflects both historical changes in the language plus a good deal of corruption of the names, often a result of a lack of understanding of their meaning as English replaced Cornish as the main language of communication.

It is generally considered appropriate today to use the Cornish form of the name when speaking or writing in the Cornish language and the form found on the map when speaking English.

◊ ◊ ◊ ◊ ◊ ◊

2a. Nouns denoting a habitation or settlement:

Cornish	found spelt as	meaning	examples
-ji -ti	suffixed -jy, -dy, -gy, -ty	building, house	Melinji (*Mellengy*) millhouse Leti (*Laity*) milkhouse, dairy
bos	bos, bo, bod,	dwelling (often followed by a personal name)	Boskarn (*Boscarn*) dwelling by the rockpile Boskennek (*Boconnoc*) Connoc's house
chi	chy, ty, che, chi	building, house	Chivarghas (*Chyvarghas*) market house Chigwynn (*Chegwin*) white house
godrevi	godrevy	small farms	Godrevi (*Godrevy*) small farms
kar, ker	car, cr, gear	fort, town	Karvedh (*Carveth*) fort of the grave
lann	la, lam, land,	holy enclosure (often followed by name of a saint)	Lannlogh (*Landlooe*) enclosure by inlet Lannwenep (*Gwennap*) Gwennep's enclosure
tre	tre, dre, drea, dra	farm, settlement	Trewartha (*Trewartha*) upper farm
tre an	tren, trem	the farm of the	Trengov (*Trengove*) farm of the smith
trev	trev	farm, settlement	Trevosker (*Treviscoe*) Osker's farm
trev an	tren, trem	the farm of the	Trenkrug (*Trencreek*) farm by barrow

◊ ◊ ◊ ◊ ◊

2b. Nouns denoting man made features:

Cornish	found spelt as*	meaning	examples
bal	bal	mine working	Baldu (*Baldhu*) black mine
din, dinas	dun, deen, dennis, dinnis, den, dem, deen, dine, dom	hillfort	Penndinas (*Pendennis*) headland with fort
eglos	eglos, iglas	church	Eglosheyl (*Egloshayle*) church by estuary Treveglos (*Treviglas*) church farm
fordh	fr, for, vor	road	Trefordhow (*Trevorrow*) farm by roads
fos	vose, voss, voes, vos, furs, vase	wall, dike	Trefos (*Trevose*) farm by/with a wall
gwel	gwel, gweal, gal, gul, gwoal	arable field	Chi an Gwel (*Chyangweal*) house by a field
hwel	huel, wheal, hu	mine	Hwel Maria (*Wheal Mary*) Mary's mine
krows	growse, grouse, crows	cross	Trengrows (*Trengrouse*) farm by a cross
krug	creek, creeg, creak, crug, crig, greek, creg, crege	barrow, mound	Roskrug (*Rosekruge*) down with a barrow Krug an Fos (*Creak a Vose*) barrow by a dike
lys	lis, les, liz, lease	court	Lysardh (*Lizard*) high court
marghas	maras, maraz, market, marz	market	Marghasvyghan (*Marazion*) little market
melin	mellan vellen, velyn, vellan, melion, miling, vellyn, mellon	mill	Pollvelin (*Polvelyn*) mill by the pool
merther	merther, medda	martyr, chapel	Merther (*Merther*) chapel of martyr
park	park, parc	field	Parknowydh (*Parknoweth*) new field
pons	pons, pont, ponds, pon	bridge	Pennpons (*Penponds*) bridge end

* this is by no means an exhaustive list of variant forms found

◇ ◇ ◇ ◇ ◇

2c. Nouns denoting natural features:

Cornish	found spelt as*	meaning	examples
bre	brea, vrea, fra, bray, frey, fry	hill	Kellivre (Kelly Bray) copse by a hill
bronn	burn, brown, barn, borne	hill	Bronnwennili (Brown Willy) hill of swallows
fenten	venton, fenter, fenton, venta	spring	Trefenten (Trefenton) farm with a spring
goen	goen, goon, oon, woone, noon, gun, gon, woon	downland	Goenhyli (Goonhilly) salty down
hal	hal, hale	moor	Halwynn (Halwyn) whitemoor
heyl	hayle, hel, hell	estuary	Heyl (Hayle) estuary
karn	carn, carne, cairne	rockpile, tor	Karnbre (Carn Brea) hill with tor
karrek	garrack, carrick	rock	An Garrek (Angarrack) the rock
kelli	kelly, gelly, calla, gilly, killy, colli	copse	Penn an Gelli (Pengelly) end of the copse
koes	cuit, cot, quite, coys, coose, goose, cus, gos cott, choys, cut coise, gus, cos	wood	Koesheyl (Cotehele) wood on estuary Melingoes (Mellancoose) mill by a wood
logh	looe, loe. lo, low, lowe, lu	inlet, pool	Nanslogh (Nansloe) valley with an inlet
lynn	lyn, lidden, land, linn, le, lan, lin	lake, pool	Lynnmargh (Lemar) horse pool Syghlynn (Sellan) dry pool
men	men, mean, ven, meyne, maen, mayne, maine	stone	Menskrifa (Menscryfa) stone with writing
menydh	mena, vena, menner, menor, venner, venna, veneth	mountain	Goenvenydh (Gunvena) down on mountain Trevenydh (Trevenna) farm on mountain
nans	nans, nance, lant, lan, lam, nan, nant, nett	valley	Nanseglos (Lanteglos) valley with church Nansmeur (Nancemeor) big valley
penn	pen, pedn.	head	Pennsans (Penzance) holy head

A backgroud to Cornish   *The formation of place names*

penntir	pentire	headland	**Penntir Glas** (*Pentire Glaze*) grey headland
poll	*poll, pol. pool, pull, bole*	pool, pit	**Pennpoll** (*Penpoll*) head of the pool
porth	*porth, por, par, pr*	cove, harbour, gateway	**Porthskathow** (*Portscatho*) cove boats
ros	*rose, res, roose, rowse, tres, ras*	heath	**Rosdowrek** (*Rostowrack*) watery heath
rys	*rit, red, tres, led rice, rid, re*	ford	**Pennrys** (*Penrice*) head of the ford
tewynn	*towan, tewan, tewing*	sand hill, dune	**Porthtewynn** (*Porthtowan*) cove with dunes
tonn	*ton, todn, dodden*	grassland	**Chitonn** (*Chytodden*) house on grassland
treth	*treath, dreath*	sand, beach	**Porthtreth** (*Portreath*) cove with a beach
ynys	*ennis, nennis, enys, ince, innis*	island, isolated place	**Porthynys** (*Mousehole*) cove by an island **Goenynys** (*Innes Down*) isolated down

* this is by no means an exhaustive list of variant forms found.

◊ ◊ ◊ ◊ ◊ ◊

2d. Common adjectives in place names:

Cornish	found spelt as*	meaning	examples
byghan	bean, vean, pian, bicon, biggan, vine, pean, beigh, biffin, beacon, byan,	small, little	Porthbyghan (*Porthpean*) little cove
-ek	-ock, -ick, -ack, -ec	place where something is grown or found	Seviek (*Sheviock*) strawberry field Stenek (*Stennack*) tin bearing ground
glas	las, glaze, glase, laze, glese	green, blue, grey	Karnglas (*Carnglaze*) grey rock
goeles	gullas, gollas, wollas	bottom, lower	Trewoeles (*Trewollas*) lower farm
gwartha	gwartha, wartha	top, higher	Andrewartha (*Andrewartha*) the higher farm
gwynn	gwyn, gwen, wyn, wen, widden, quidden, win, whidden	white, fair	Porthgwynn (*Portquin*) fair harbour
hen	hen	old, ancient	Henlys (*Helston*) ancient court
hir	heere, heer, hire	long	Menhir (*Menheere*) long stone
kompes	gumpus	smooth, level	Goengompes (*Woon Gumpes*) level moor
meur	mear, meor, vear, veor, meer, mere, maer	great, large	Porthmeur (*Porthmear*) big cove
nowydh	noweth, nowah, nouth, nuth, nower, nowith,	new	Chinowydh (*Chynooth*) new house
rudh	ruth, reath, reeth	red	Rysrudh (*Redruth*) red ford
sans	zant, zance, sent, zens	holy	Lannsans (*Lezant*) holy enclosure
sygh	zeath, seath, sig, suff, shea, zeth	dry	Pollsygh (*Polzeath*) dry pool
war	war, var, ver	on	Chi war Dreth (*Tywardreath*) house on beach
yeyn	eyn, ine, yon,	cold	Nansyeyn (*Lanyon*) cold valley
ynn	edn, idden, idne	narrow	Trevynn (*Treveddon*) narrow farm

* this is by no means an exhaustive list of variant forms found.

The above examples and principles are a very brief outline guide and introduction to a very complex subject. Many Cornish place names still defy certain interpretation and debates will rage on in other instances. It is always necessary to look at old forms of each name, from maps or documents, to see how it has evolved through time.

For those using the Cornish language, however, it is vital that Cornish forms are available, even if sometimes they may need to be re-interpreted in the future should new evidence come to light. This is the situation in other bilingual countries, including all the other five Celtic countries.

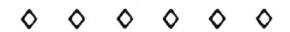

◊ ◊ ◊ ◊ ◊ ◊

What is very clear in even a brief study of place names in Cornwall is that the vast majority are of Cornish, Celtic stock. Cornish is the predominant language in place names throughout Cornwall from the Land's End to the Tamar. Indeed the Tamar makes a near perfect linguistic boundary.

Further research is necessary and further publications will emerge to develop and supplement these ideas. Workers such as Oliver Padel in Cornwall and Anthony Lais in Wales have developed formulae for academic study and longer lists of Cornish recommended names are in preparation.

Other booklets in this series examine various aspects of the background to our Cornish language which will be of interest to Cornish people and to students of the language.

A background to Cornish, number one:
Place-names in Cornwall by
Ken George, Pol Hodge, Julyan Holmes & Graham Sandercock

A background to Cornish, number three:
A very brief history of the Cornish language by
Graham Sandercock

◊ ◊ ◊ ◊ ◊ ◊